Unlocking the Secrets of Science

Profiling 20th Century Achievers in Science, Medicine, and Technology

Wilhelm Roentgen and the Discovery of X Rays

Kimberly Garcia

Mitchell Lane **PUBLISHERS**

PO Box 619
Bear, Delaware 19701

Unlocking the Secrets of Science

Profiling 20th Century Achievers in Science, Medicine, and Technology

Marc Andreessen and the Development of the Web Browser

Frederick Banting and the Discovery of Insulin

Jonas Salk and the Polio Vaccine

Wallace Carothers and the Story of DuPont Nylon

Tim Berners-Lee and the Development of the World Wide Web

Robert A. Weinberg and the Search for the Cause of Cancer

Alexander Fleming and the Story of Penicillin

Robert Goddard and the Liquid Rocket Engine

Oswald Avery and the Story of DNA

Edward Teller and the Development of the Hydrogen Bomb

Stephen Wozniak and the Story of Apple Computer

Barbara McClintock: Pioneering Geneticist

Wilhelm Roentgen and the Discovery of X Rays

Gerhard Domagk and the Discovery of Sulfa

Willem Kolff and the Invention of the Dialysis Machine

Robert Jarvik and the First Artificial Heart

Chester Carlson and the Development of Xerography

Joseph E. Murray and the Story of the First Human Kidney Transplant

Albert Einstein and the Theory of Relativity

Edward Roberts and the Story of the Personal Computer

Godfrey Hounsfield and the Invention of CAT Scans

Christaan Barnard and the Story of the First Successful Heart Transplant

Selman Waksman and the Discovery of Streptomycin

Paul Ehrlich and Modern Drug Development

Sally Ride: The Story of the First Female in Space

Luis Alvarez and the Development of the Bubble Chamber

Jacques-Yves Cousteau: His Story Under the Sea

Francis Crick and James Watson: Pioneers in DNA Research

Raymond Damadian and the Development of the Open MRI

Wilhelm Roentgen and the Discovery of X Rays

First Printing

Library of Congress Cataloging-in-Publication Data
Garcia, Kimberly, 1966-
    Wilhelm Roentgen and the discovery of x rays/Kimberly Garcia.
       p. cm. — (Unlocking the secrets of science)
    Includes bibliographical references and index.
    Summary: Presents the biography of the German scientist Wilhelm Roentgen and the story of how he discovered x rays.
    ISBN 1-58415-114-5
    1. Rèntgen, Wilhelm Conrad, 1845-1923—Juvenile literature. 2. X rays—Juvenile literature. 3. Physicists—Germany—Biography—Juvenile literature. [1. Rèntgen, Wilhelm Conrad, 1845-1923. 2. Physicists. 3. X rays] I. Title. II. Series.
QC16.R47 G37 2002
530'.092—dc21
    [B]   2001050449

ABOUT THE AUTHOR: Kimberly Garcia is a bilingual journalist who found her first job at a newspaper on the U.S.- Mexico border because she spoke Spanish. Her paternal great grandparents migrated from Spain in the early 1900s to New York where her great grandfather edited an Anarchist newspaper. Garcia has a bachelor's degree in English and Spanish literature from the University of Wisconsin in Madison. After graduation, she worked for six years as a daily newspaper journalist covering crime, local governments and Hispanic-related issues in Texas and Wisconsin. Garcia writes for *Hispanic*, *Vista*, and *Latina* magazines, among other publications. She currently lives in Austin, Texas.

PHOTO CREDITS: cover: Bill Sanderson/Science Photo Library; p. 9 AP Pholo/File; p. 12 Science Photo Library; p. 18 Science Photo Library; p. 25 AP Photo; p. 26 AP Photo; p. 32 J. L. Charmet/Science Photo Library; p. 38 GE Medical PR NewsPhoto.

PUBLISHER'S NOTE: In selecting those persons to be profiled in this series, we first attempted to identify the most notable accomplishments of the 20th century in science, medicine, and technology. When we were done, we noted a serious deficiency in the inclusion of women. For the greater part of the 20th century science, medicine, and technology were male-dominated fields. In many cases, the contributions of women went unrecognized. Women have tried for years to be included in these areas, and in many cases, women worked side by side with men who took credit for their ideas and discoveries. Even as we move forward into the 21st century, we find women still sadly underrepresented. It is not an oversight, therefore, that we profiled mostly male achievers. Information simply does not exist to include a fair selection of women.

Contents

Wilhelm Conrad Roentgen, who discovered x rays, is shown in this undated picture. The x ray remains one of the greatest advances in the history of medicine. Today, x rays are also used to authenticate paintings, stamps, and coins, and in quality control laboratories to check the manufacture of countless products.

Chapter 1

An Invisible Discovery

• •

A popular TV series that began during the 1950s began with the words "Look up in the air. It's a bird. It's a plane. No, it's Superman!"

It continued with a list of Superman's attributes: "Faster than a speeding bullet! More powerful that a speeding locomotive! Able to leap tall buildings in a single bound!"

And then there was Superman's x ray vision. In many of the episodes, a cone of light would come from his eyes so he could peer through the solid walls of a building or the container of a mysterious package to determine what dangers might lurk inside.

While most of Superman's other powers were products of the cartoonist's imagination, his x ray vision was a quality that was based solidly on fact.

By the time Superman made his television debut, people had been familiar with x rays for over half a century. A form of energy that penetrates materials such as skin and paper, but not others such as bones and certain kinds of metal, x rays are important in many real ways aside from Superman's fictitious adventures. They improve our health by helping doctors look inside our bodies for broken bones or harmful growths such as cancer. They protect our safety by helping security workers see inside packages or suitcases to keep dangerous devices out of airplanes and public buildings. And they are becoming increasingly important as astronomers seek the mysteries of the universe.

When Wilhelm Roentgen discovered x rays more than 100 years ago, he had no idea how the rays would be used and how radically those uses would improve our lives. In fact, Roentgen stumbled on x rays by accident when working late one November night in 1895 in his laboratory in Würzburg, Germany. Then 50 years old, he was a physical scientist who was experimenting with electricity.

Scientists back then were just beginning to understand the properties of electricity in an attempt to harness its power. They experimented with sealed glass tubes from which almost all the air had been removed. Two wires connected to a generator were inserted into the tube, one at each end. One of these wires—the negative pole—was called a cathode, while the other—the positive pole—was known as the anode.

When the power source was turned on, a stream of charged particles would travel from the cathode to the anode. These particles were known as cathode rays and scientists began studying them in earnest. They knew a cathode ray could travel through thin sheets of metal such as aluminum. They also knew that cathode rays could travel only a few inches past the tube before they disappeared... into thin air. Roentgen wanted to find out if cathode rays could travel through glass.

On that fateful night, he applied a powerful current of electricity to a vacuum tube wrapped in a shield of black cardboard. He knew cathode rays caused a glow of color when they came in contact with air. If the rays could travel through glass, the glow of color would light up the tube. The results of his query were not startling. The tube did not light up, so Roentgen concluded that cathode rays could not travel through glass.

But he noticed something out of the ordinary. A thin cardboard screen treated with a chemical called barium platinocyanide lying on a table several feet away was glowing. Mystified, he turned off the electrical current that had been flowing into the tube. The glowing stopped. He turned the current back on. The glowing returned.

So he began moving the screen. The closer he got to the vacuum tube, the brighter it glowed. The further he moved the screen from the tube, the fainter the glow became. It appeared that somehow the tube was projecting an invisible light on to the screen. The crystals of barium platinocyanide made the light visible.

The observation intrigued Roentgen so he investigated further. He held a thin sheet of paper between the tube and the screen, and the screen still glowed. Then he held up a book. Same result. Testing again, he replaced the book with a double pack of cards, a single sheet of tinfoil, a thick block of wood, pine boards, glass plates, fabric, liquids. Every time he found the same results. The screen still glowed. It appeared this invisible light could travel through certain materials.

But what was this invisible light? It couldn't be cathode rays. They couldn't penetrate the glass tube walls. Even if they could, they disappeared after traveling a couple of inches.

Nor could it be visible light. The room itself lay in darkness with the shades drawn. And the tube was covered with black paper.

Therefore, Roentgen concluded, "I have discovered some new form of light ray."

But what was really surprising happened when Roentgen held up his hand between the tube and screen. The scientist was shocked to see the bones and joints in his hand. The implications were staggering.

He also took a photograph to document his results. Other scientists had discovered that cathode rays would darken photographic plates when leaving a vacuum tube. So Roentgen wrapped a photographic plate in black paper, placed it where the screen had been lying, and repeated his experiment. Sure enough, the invisible light darkened the plate. The photograph gave Wilhelm proof of his discovery.

"This is a new kind of invisible light," Roentgen wrote in his notebook. "It is clearly new, something unrecorded."

For the time being, he called the invisible light "x rays" because scientists use the letter "x" to stand for the unknown.

Despite his proof, he kept quiet about his discovery. The meticulous scientist wanted to run and rerun his experiment, as was his habit, to be absolutely sure of its accuracy before sharing his findings with others. He worked non-stop for several weeks, isolating himself from others, often eating and sometimes sleeping on a cot in his laboratory.

He had his wife place her hand on a photographic plate for 15 minutes while the x rays passed through it. The resulting picture became famous. Her flesh and muscles are virtually transparent as the x rays easily traveled through them. The bones appear much darker, while her wedding ring, having absorbed virtually all the rays, shows up as a solid image.

By the end of December, he was ready to release the news of his revolutionary discovery to the world. So he gave a preliminary paper to an officer of the Physical Society of Würzburg. He also submitted a paper, called "A New Kind of Ray," that was published in a scientific journal. Wilhelm's final dissemination came on New Year's Day when he mailed copies of the report to recognized physicists, including some personal friends.

One of these friends, University of Vienna professor Franz Exner, became the vehicle for spreading the news like wildfire around the world when he shared the report with colleagues. One of them was Ernst Lecher, a young assistant professor from Prague. Lecher immediately rushed to the office of his father, who was editor of *The Presse*, a daily newspaper in Vienna. When the newspaper broke the story about x rays in the January 5, 1896 edition, publications around the world spread the news. Roentgen's discovery rocked the world, as well as his private life.

"On January first I sent out the first off prints and then all hell broke lose," he wrote in a letter to a friend. "*The Presse* in Vienna was the first to blast the trumpet to the world and the others followed. After a few weeks, I was disgusted with the whole thing. I could not even recognize my own work on reading the reports. Photography was only a means to me and yet this was made the main discovery. Slowly I got used to all the racket, but the storm cost time; I could not do a single experiment for four full weeks. Other people could do work—but I could not. You have no idea what went on."

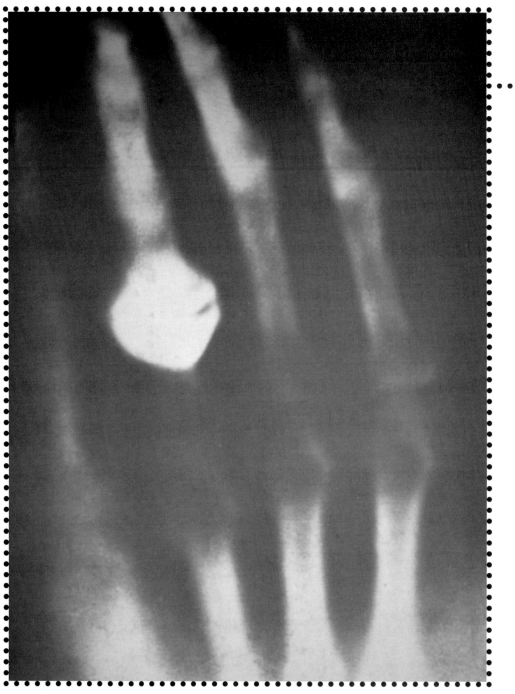

This famous photograph is the first x ray ever made of a human being. Roentgen made it of his wife's hand shortly after his discovery of x rays. You can see the ring on her finger.

Chapter 2

Losing His Lead on Life

Wilhelm Conrad Roentgen was born into a life of prosperity and good fortune on March 27, 1845. His parents, Friedrich and Charlotte, lived in an attractive frame house in Lennep, Prussia, which is part of modern-day Germany. Charlotte came from a line of successful merchants and tradespeople. She was raised in the central Netherlands, but frequently visited her grandparents and other close relatives in Lennep. There, she met and married her first cousin Friedrich, as was common in small villages in those days. A successful cloth manufacturer and retailer who was skilled in using his hands, Friedrich worked alongside up to 20 employees who operated looms in his workshop.

Despite the Roentgens' strong economic standing, the authorities governing Prussia created an uncertain climate for Friedrich's business. Wilhelm was three years old in 1848 when the difficulty caused the family to move to Charlotte's hometown of Apeldoorn, Holland, nearly 160 miles from Lennep. Though the move cost Friedrich his Prussian citizenship, he soon became a Dutch citizen. The family remained in Apeldoorn for decades, finding success and comfort among the hospitable Dutch people.

More than 10,000 people lived in Apeldoorn back then. Many of them were farmers, cattle breeders, sheep raisers, or workers in one of the city's 40 paper mills. The Roentgens lived in a comfortable home adorned with some of the fine furnishings Charlotte's family had acquired during their travels. Wedgwood and Meissen china lined the cupboards along with silver hollowware and old Chinese porcelain. Mahogany Empire furniture and 18th century chairs graced the sitting rooms while fine Dutch paintings, including an art treasure of the Holy Family, were hung on the walls.

In addition, Friedrich added his handiwork to the family heirlooms. Among his creations was an elaborate replica of their previous home in Lennep, complete with slate roof, slate tile siding and a stone walkway to the front door. The model could be disassembled to expose the home's rooms, and Wilhelm kept it throughout his life. Friedrich was particularly inventive at Christmas time when he made a nativity scene, a creche and a small wooden windmill run by fine sand.

As a child, Wilhelm's life in Apeldoorn was enriching both inside and outside his home. He loved nature and learning. Some of his favorite outdoor activities were exploring the thick forests surrounding Apeldoorn, taking a dip in swimming holes in the picturesque Grift river and ice skating on the Dieren Canal.

Wilhelm also enjoyed school. Initially, he attended a public primary school. Later, he transferred to a private boarding school close to his home. His parents paid nearly $95 a year to send their son to the Institute of Martinus Hermann van Doorn, then considered the best school in Apeldoorn. Wilhelm mastered the alphabet early and reading followed easily. He also found satisfaction in working with numbers and in finding answers to many of the questions that poured through his mind.

Wilhelm even showed a propensity for mechanical gadgets when he began smoking cigars at age 15, as was the custom for Dutch boys. Wilhelm's uncle gave him a mouthpiece for smoking cigars, and added a warning that the piece would give off an unpleasant taste during the first couple of uses. To avoid that bad taste, Wilhelm created a suction pump for the mouthpiece that smoked the first few cigars for him.

By the time Wilhelm was 16 years old, he had exhausted all the educational opportunities appropriate for him in Apeldoorn. It was customary at that time for sons—especially only sons, as Wilhelm was—to help with their parents' work and eventually take it over. But Wilhelm's parents decided to provide him with more education, so they sent him to attend the Technical School of Utrecht. Utrecht was a city of nearly 100,000 people that was located about 40 miles west of Apeldoorn. The two-year curriculum provided a technical background for future factory managers, as well as classes in modern languages such as Dutch, English, German, and French. The school also granted high school graduation certificates that were required to enter college.

When Wilhelm enrolled, nearly 60 students attended the school. Because of the distance from his home, Wilhelm had to find accommodations with a local family. So he was warmly welcomed into the home of Jan Willem Gunning, a chemistry professor at the University of Utrecht who also taught at Wilhelm's school.

Living with other children was a pleasant experience for Wilhelm, who had grown up without any siblings. Gunning's wife, Elis, became like a second mother, and one of their children, a daughter named Jo, became Wilhelm's companion in mischief and adventure. He also shared the family's grief when a two-year-old daughter died and their joy when a son was born. Wilhelm fondly recalled his stay with the Gunnings in a letter 45 years later to Margret Boveri, the young daughter of a colleague.

"The father of this family was a fine scholar, a solid character, and really a splendid man who understood superbly the task of guiding a young person along the correct path in several areas in life," he wrote. "The mother was a loving, cultured, and kindly woman who provided the proper atmosphere for a full life, one of happiness and at the same time pleasant stimulation. There was no time for foolish and stupid things, but much for creative activities. Self-created pieces of happy fun were offered at community celebrations, but otherwise diligent work was demanded in serious learning. That was a happy and equally rewarding time!"

That same letter also revealed his lifelong love of physical exercise. "I must add that I did much horseback riding, skating, and generally exercised my body well," he said.

At first all was fine at school as his grades ranged from "good" to "excellent" for nearly two years. But an unfortunate incident at school in the spring of 1864 brought his youthful optimism to an abrupt end and complicated his educational pursuits for much of his life. A fellow student drew an unflattering caricature of an unpopular teacher on the blackboard. Wilhelm was laughing heartily when the teacher walked into the class and discovered the drawing.

The angry man blamed Wilhelm, even though he had never shown any artistic talent. Wilhelm denied responsibility, but refused to name the culprit. That denial further enraged the teacher, who then called in the school's stern director, Professor van Tweer. Van Tweer settled the dispute by handing Wilhelm an unreasonably tough punishment—he kicked the boy out of school.

As disappointed as his parents were, they stood behind their son, particularly Wilhelm's mother who believed in the principles of courtesy and decency. Unfortunately, Wilhelm paid dearly for upholding his principles. His expulsion temporarily derailed his educational plans. Without an all-important high school graduation certificate, he could not achieve his dream of obtaining a college degree. The young Wilhelm felt confused, angry and lost.

This is a photograph of the Physical Institute of Würzburg University in Germany, where Roentgen discovered x rays in 1895. This photograph was taken in 1896. Roentgen was a professor of physics at Würzburg. In a laboratory in this building he experimented with x rays in vacuum tubes.

Chapter 3

The Ups and Downs of Education

● ●

Wilhelm's first attempt to get back on an educational track involved taking a special entrance examination that would admit him to the University of Utrecht even without a high school graduation certificate. Wilhelm studied nearly a year for the exam, but the mishap at the Technical School of Utrecht continued to plague him. Teachers from his former school were on the committee that administered the exam. One of them was a teacher who liked Wilhelm, but that teacher became gravely ill. His replacement was the very same teacher whose caricature had resulted in Wilhelm's dismissal. Not surprisingly, Wilhelm was one of just two students who failed the exam among the eight who took it. Once again, his hard work fell in vain. Wilhelm wrote of his distaste for exams some 40 years later when he was a university professor in Munich, Germany.

"Student examinations generally give no clues whatever for the judgment of ability in a special field," he explained. "They are entirely—and unfortunately—a necessary evil. Especially final examinations! They are necessary to keep one from a lifetime profession for which he is too lazy or otherwise unsuited, although that is not always the case. Otherwise, they are a trial for both parties, and they cause repeatedly bad dreams! The real test of ability of any chosen profession or occupation comes actually much later in life."

Despite failing the exam, Wilhelm pressed on. He decided to attend the University of Utrecht by auditing classes, which allowed him to sit in without receiving any official credit. He registered in January 1865 as a private student of philosophy, and attended classes from May until October of 1865, even though he was not eligible to seek a degree without a high school graduation certificate.

But going to classes wasn't the only thing that occupied his time. He began writing, and soon published a 58-page book called *Questions for the Inorganic Part of the Chemistry Textbook*. This was the first of dozens of books and scholarly articles that he would produce during his life.

It now seemed more and more apparent to the young man that he wanted to have an academic career. Unfortunately he kept running into the same problem: because he didn't have his high school diploma, he couldn't get a college degree. But without a college degree, he couldn't have his academic career.

Good fortune eventually came Wilhelm's way when he made the acquaintance of Carl Ludwig Wilhelm Thormann, whose father was a locomotive engineer in Switzerland. Thormann made Wilhelm aware that a student without a high school graduation certificate could seek a degree from the Federal Institute of Technology in Zurich—Switzerland's largest city—by passing a painfully stiff entrance exam.

Another entrance exam. What did Wilhelm have to lose? Even though the classes would be conducted in a language known as High German, with which Wilhelm wasn't as comfortable as Dutch, he felt confident that he could succeed. His parents supported his decision, even though he would be much further from home. In addition, it meant even more time before Wilhelm would be able to help out his father in the family business—now, perhaps he never would. Nonetheless, Friedrich willingly agreed to provide the necessary finances if his son was admitted.

So Wilhelm wrote to the institute for permission to take the exam and enclosed his university report card that revealed his excellent grades, especially in mathematics. As he waited for a reply, he contracted an eye infection that eventually worked in his favor. The director of the institute, Gustav Zeuner, wrote back granting Wilhelm acceptance without taking the exam.

Zeuner's own professional difficulties made him sympathetic to Wilhelm's plight. Zeuner was denied employment in his birthplace of Chemnitz in Saxony because he participated in an uprising of radical liberals in 1849. So he decided to accept Wilhelm based on three reasons: his excellent grades, his mature age of 20 being two years older than other beginning students, and the eye ailment. Finally, the young man had received a break.

Arriving in Zurich, Wilhelm marveled at the rugged beauty of the nearby Swiss Alps and took up mountain climbing. He quickly made friends, who called him "Apeldoorn" because of his Dutch hometown, and enjoyed playing pranks or passing time in cafés. His favorite café was Zum Grunen Glas where in 1866 he met the woman who would eventually become his wife.

Anna Bertha Ludwig was six years older than Wilhelm and the middle daughter of the café's owner. She was tall, slender and bright with a twinkle in her eyes and a constant smile on her face. What most drew Wilhelm to her was her willingness to laugh and enjoy life. Wilhelm himself was a tall, agile man with a long beard and thick wavy hair. He sported lively brown eyes, a vigorous stride and occasionally a quick temper.

Wilhelm's time in Zurich passed quickly while he enjoyed taking classes, mostly in mathematics, chemistry and physics. By the time he graduated in 1868 with a degree in mechanical engineering, he was sure of one thing. He wanted to marry Bertha. The two became engaged while Wilhelm grappled with choosing a vocation. His interest and aptitude were for science, but he was uncertain how he could make money in the field.

Fortunately, Professor August Eduard Eberhard Kundt came into Wilhelm Roentgen's life. Kundt, 29, was an up-and-coming physicist who served as chairman of physics for the institute. His brilliant lectures on the theory of light intrigued Wilhelm, and his leadership eventually became a guiding influence in his student's life.

Kundt recommended that Wilhelm pursue a doctorate degree in physics. That boost strengthened Wilhelm's resolve to continue his education, despite the fact that he lacked a high school graduation certificate. Wilhelm did not bother applying to the University of Zurich. He knew from past experience he would not be accepted. Instead, he learned he could obtain a doctorate degree from the university if he produced "a sufficiently good thesis on a scientific subject."

Wilhelm had just such a thesis in mind. He had done research trying to find the characteristics of gases such as oxygen and nitrogen during his last year at the institute. He turned this work into a dissertation called "Studies on Gas," handed it over to university officials, and waited, once again, for word about his academic future. On June 22, 1869, a committee of professors unanimously agreed to grant Wilhelm Roentgen a doctorate degree of philosophy. One professor wrote that his work contained "more than adequate proof of very sound knowledge and a gift for independent research in the field of mathematical physics."

The accomplishment made his future ripe with possibility. Kundt was the first to snatch up his former student's abilities by offering him a job as a laboratory assistant. Roentgen jumped at the opportunity to continue investigating and experimenting under such an inspiring guide. The two worked well together and created an enduring relationship built on mutual respect for ingenuity, precision and reclusive work habits.

In fact, Roentgen followed Kundt's career for a decade as his mentor moved among several institutions. He served as Kundt's first assistant when Kundt became chairman of physics in the fall of 1870 at the University of Würzburg in Germany. Not long afterward, Kundt left the university. Part of the reason was the authorities' refusal to make Roentgen a professor because he lacked the ominous high school graduation certificate. Instead, the pair moved to the University of Strasbourg, where more agreeable authorities promised to support Roentgen's quest to become a professor.

Early in 1872, shortly before the move to Strasbourg, Roentgen married Bertha at his parents' home in Apeldoorn. Thormann stood as Wilhelm's best man at the festive occasion packed with guests. Unfortunately, the new bridegroom's meager earnings as a laboratory assistant put a strain on wedded life. He took a brief post in 1875 as a professor of mathematics and physics at the Agricultural

Academy of Hohenheim, but inadequate laboratory equipment, uncomfortable living conditions and longing for their old friends drove the young couple back to Strasbourg a year later. Finally, Roentgen secured a job with Kundt as an associate professor of physics.

Back in Strasbourg, developments continued in his personal and work lives. His parents retired, and came to live with Bertha and him in the late 1870s. About the same time, doctors determined Bertha could not bear children, much to her and her husband's dismay. Meanwhile, Roentgen continued working diligently and carving out of a niche of creating laboratory equipment when existing equipment did not meet his needs, and of developing a reputation for obsessively checking and rechecking both his own work and that of others.

His growing reputation caught the attention in 1879 of the authorities at Germany's University of Giessen. They offered him a job as director of the physical institute and professor of physics as the time had finally come for Roentgen to step out from Kundt's shadow.

His parents followed him and Bertha to his new position. They eventually passed away, Charlotte in 1880 at age 74 and Friedrich in 1884 at age 83. Both are buried in Giessen. A blessing also came to Wilhelm and Bertha in Giessen. Bertha's brother, Hans, sent his six-year-old daughter, Josephine Bertha Ludwig, to the couple in 1881 to love and to raise as their own. By then, Roentgen was earning enough money to travel and enjoy life with his small family.

An ironic twist in his advancing career as a professor came in 1888. Both the universities of Utrecht and Würzburg offered him professorships. These were the very same universities that had previously denied him educational opportunities because he lacked the all-important high school graduation certificate.

Roentgen chose the post in Würzburg, where he remained for 12 years. He became director in 1894, the same year Kundt died while recovering from illness at his summer home outside Lübeck. And the following year he made the discovery that would make him world-famous.

This is a photograph of the laboratory in which Roentgen conducted his experiments at the University of Würzburg. This photograph was taken about 50 years after his discovery (1945).

Wilhelm II, former emperor of Germany and king of Prussia between 1888-1918, is shown here in uniform in Doorn, Netherland, 1930. In 1896, Wilhelm II commanded Roentgen to give a demonstration of his x rays before the royal family.

Chapter 4
A World Turned Upside Down

Roentgen's discovery of x rays sent his own life and the world around him into a tailspin. As news about x rays traveled around the world, an unwelcome amount of attention suffocated him. Letters and requests for interviews and demonstrations of his experiment poured in from scientists, journalists, royalty and presidents around the world. Roentgen tried to deflect the queries as much as possible, but some people were not easy to put off.

Among them was Wilhelm II, the German emperor. Wilhelm II commanded Roentgen to give a demonstration before the royal family and the German court at Potsdam on January 13, 1896. The Kaiser was so intrigued with Roentgen's work that he kept the scientist at the court until past midnight answering questions. The Kaiser also decorated Roentgen with the Prussian Order of the Crown, Second Class.

Another one of the few audiences Roentgen agreed to address was the Physical Medical Society of Würzburg. Again, Roentgen wowed the audience, whose members included Albert Rudolf von Kölliker, a renowned professor of anatomy and head of the medical school in Würzburg. Roentgen took an x ray of Kölliker's hand during the January 23, 1896 meeting. Kölliker extolled Roentgen's research and suggested that the new rays be called Roentgen's rays in honor of their discoverer. The modest Roentgen declined.

One reason was that while he could not help but appreciate the praise, he did not think the discovery belonged entirely to him. In fact, he disagreed with suggestions that he capitalize financially on x rays by taking out a patent on the discovery or a copyright on the first x ray pictures he took. A patent is an exclusive right that a government gives an inventor for a certain period of time to make, use or sell his discovery. Roentgen could have made himself rich by selling copies of his x ray pictures and the right to use his discovery.

Instead, Roentgen credited his predecessors' work as much as his own for the discovery. After all, other scientists produced x rays long before Roentgen. Francis Hauksbee might have been the first to produce the rays in the early 1700s when he observed glow discharges during experiments with a vacuum tube. Abbé Jean Nollet also may have produced x rays in the late 1700s while experimenting with an electrical egg. Several German scientists in the late 1800s made similar observations. But no one understood what they observed until Roentgen.

So Roentgen thought his discovery belonged to the world, as he told Max Levy of the German Electric Company, AEG. "According to the good tradition of the German university professors, I am of the opinion that their discoveries and inventions belong to humanity and that they should not in any way be hampered by patents, licenses, contracts, nor should they be controlled by any one group," he explained.

Indeed, the world grabbed on to its entitled share of Roentgen's discovery and worked furiously to capitalize on the advantages of x rays. A London physician was among the first to administer a medical application of x rays. One of his patients was a sailor who came to the hospital drunk with a small bleeding wound on his back. The man was unable to walk, talk or grasp with his hands, and attempts to cure him were not successful. So the physician took an x ray of the sailor's back, which showed a foreign body between two of the vertebrae. The physician made an incision at this point and removed a small knife blade. The next day the sailor could walk.

Another early use of x rays for healing came from two brothers in the United States. Doctors Gilman and Edwin Frost used x rays to find the break in a patient's arm on February 3, 1896 at Dartmouth College in Hanover, New Hampshire. The information helped the brothers reset the arm.

Other early users of x rays were not as benevolent. Thomas Edison, a U.S. inventor of electrical devices, learned of Roentgen's discovery two days after the news reached North America. He quickly set out to make money on the discovery and within four days had repeated all of Roentgen's experiments. Edison and his staff worked 72 hours without stopping to find a better screening device for x rays than barium platinocyanide plates. They tested more than 1,200 chemical compounds and found that calcium tungstate provided the brightest pictures. Edison then created a fluoroscope to view objects exposed to x rays. The device consisted of a tube or box fitted with a screen coated with a fluorescent substance. Edison demonstrated his fluoroscope at the Electric Fair in New York in May 1896. Eventually, he took out a patent to cash in on his invention.

"Professor Roentgen probably does not draw one dollar profit from his discovery. He belongs to those pure scientists who study for pleasure and love to delve into the secrets of nature," Edison said. "After they have discovered something wonderful, someone else must come to look at it from the commercial point of view."

As doctors and inventors came up with new uses for x rays, scientists worldwide repeated Roentgen's experiments and searched for additional knowledge about the mysterious rays. The flurry of activity was so feverish that manufacturers of electrical equipment for x ray research could not keep up with demand. In 1896 alone, 49 books and pamphlets and 1,044 papers on x rays were published.

Some of the activity regarding x rays was downright foolish. In the United States, an Iowa farmer and graduate of Columbia University in New York claimed he could convert metal to gold by treating the metal with x rays for three hours, saying that he'd converted a piece of metal worth 13 cents into gold valued at $153. Another person suggested that x rays could beam anatomy diagrams directly into the brains of medical students, making it easier for them to learn. And there were even suggestions that x rays could see through women's clothing and therefore the "fairer sex" needed to wear x ray proof underwear.

The most significant development regarding x rays came from the work of Antoine Henri Becquerel, a French physicist. Becquerel found that x rays could travel from one body through an intervening medium to another body. This process—called radioactivity—constituted a whole new branch of physics. Before the discovery of x rays, scientists believed the study of physics was complete, except for adding more decimal points to measurements. Roentgen was proud that his discovery of x rays, or radiation, led Becquerel to uncover radioactivity and to open up the world of physics.

The worst consequence of x ray use was that people began reporting damage, mostly in the United States, from exposure to the rays. Roentgen had unknowingly protected himself from harmful rays during his later research by working inside a sheet metal box. Others were not as fortunate. In New York, x ray exposure caused several health problems for H.D. Hawks, a student who gave demonstrations of an x ray machine at Bloomingdale Brothers department store. This work soon burned his skin, caused his fingernails to stop growing, impaired his vision and caused the hair on his head, eyebrows and eyelashes to fall out. Hawks' case was mild by comparison to other cases. At least x ray exposure did not cost him his life.

One of Edison's assistants, Clarence Madison Dally, was the first person in the United States to die from overexposure to x rays. Dally was a glassblower who helped Edison with fluoroscope demonstrations at the Electric Fair in New York. He continuously exposed his arm to x rays so spectators could see his bones. As a result, Dally lost several fingers on his right hand and had to have his left hand amputated when his skin rotted away from x ray exposure. He died six years later in 1904. The damage to Dally prompted Edison to drop further x ray experiments.

So many people eventually died from early use of x rays that a stone monument was created in 1936 to memorialize them. More than 100 names have been carved on the monument at the Roentgen Institute in Hamburg, Germany. Its dedication reads, "To the roentgenologists of all nations who have given their lives in the struggle against diseases of mankind."

This cartoon was published in 1900, five years after Roentgen discovered x rays.

Chapter 5
A High Price for Fame

The effects of Roentgen's revolutionary discovery on his personal life became bittersweet, particularly as he aged. His work garnered some of the highest honors in the world and led him to a prestigious new job, but his fame eventually drove him into profound isolation, particularly after his wife died.

Roentgen began shutting his door on the world shortly after his discovery. All the attention he received frustrated his desire to return to his research. Other people's furious work on x rays also put him under pressure to continue his experiments. After all, he wanted to stay at the forefront of scientific research on x rays. Finally, Roentgen stopped returning most letters, refused requests for interviews and demonstrations, and went back to work in his laboratory.

He released a second paper on x rays in March of 1896 in the same journal that published his first paper, revealing another crucial discovery. He found that when x rays travel through air, the air becomes electrified and can discharge the charge it is carrying. Today, we call this ionization of air. In other words, Roentgen found that air was a conductor for electricity.

Roentgen released his third and final paper in March 1897. "Further Observations on the Properties of X Rays" was published this time by the Prussian Academy of Sciences in Berlin. The paper dealt with the intensity of radiation and how to measure radiation. Roentgen found by changing tubes, he could produce more or less powerful rays. He called the more powerful rays "hard rays" and the less powerful ones "soft rays." He recommended what type of rays should be used when photographing various objects. Hard rays, for example, were best for photographing bones while soft rays were best for fleshy parts of the body.

For his work, Roentgen won award after award. The most remarkable came in 1901 as Roentgen was selected to be the first Nobel Prize winner for physics. The Nobel Prize is one of the highest honors in the world. The King of Sweden presents the award annually for extraordinary accomplishments in physics, chemistry, medicine, literature and contributions to world peace. Recipients receive money from a fund created by Alfred Nobel, a Swedish millionaire who donated some of his profits from the manufacture of dynamite and other explosives to the fund in the interest of promoting world peace. As was customary for Roentgen, he shared his success with the world by donating the award to the University of Würzburg to create opportunities for scientific discoveries that would help people.

Earlier, he'd had another proud moment when he became the chairman of experimental physics and the director of the physics institute at the University of Munich in 1899. The large university in the capital of the kingdom of Bavaria made the move a prestigious step up for Roentgen. Yet he kept finding out again and again that trouble followed prestige, even when he tried to humble himself. His fame complicated efforts to make new friends in Munich.

Roentgen also got off on the wrong foot with the Bavarian minister of education, whose financial support he needed to buy laboratory equipment. The Prince Regent of

Bavaria had awarded Roentgen the Royal Bavarian Order of the Crown while Roentgen was still in Würzburg. The honor gave Roentgen the right to place "von" before his name. Because Roentgen wanted his principles and achievement to speak for themselves, rather than his titles, he declined the offer. But his refusal had offended the minister.

Roentgen wrote his friend Theodor Boveri about the incident, saying, "So many things could be beautiful and good in Munich if there were not some people who are chiefly convinced of their own importance without, however, sufficient reason. In addition to this, the minister of education is a bureaucrat and has no real interest in the development and the progress of the university, probably because he is not familiar with the conditions. It is really a miracle and a sign of great inner strength that science in Germany makes so much progress in spite of ministers and other impediments."

Life in Munich eventually became so uncomfortable that Roentgen bought a country house 40 miles southwest of Munich in the small mountain town of Weilheim in 1904. The "hunting lodge," as Roentgen called it, became the only place he could hide from his fame and relax. There, both he and Bertha could enjoy their love of the outdoors. She would collect wildflowers and tend to her garden while he would hunt or mountain climb. The home became a necessary respite during the health problems they encountered as they grew older

Roentgen had enjoyed a lifetime of robust health to that point, but he suffered an episode of vertigo in 1910 that nearly caused him to collapse during a meeting. Later, doctors discovered two hemorrhages in his lungs. Roentgen also wrestled with severe bronchitis for five weeks in 1912 and an ear inflammation soon afterward that left him with impaired hearing. Doctors operated on the ear in 1913, and Roentgen recovered without severe damage.

Bertha, on the other hand, had struggled with her health her entire life. Her kidneys became so fragile in 1913 that Roentgen had to give her five shots of a pain-killing drug called morphine each day.

The start of World War I in 1914 added to their problems. The war involving 30 nations lasted more than four years and left Germany defeated, poor and starving. While he was pleased that x rays were used to help ease the sufferings of sick and wounded soldiers and civilians, the amount of death and destruction made him profoundly sad. Even Roentgen had difficulty making ends meet, despite his good fortune of working as a professor amid the country's high unemployment. Times were made tough by Germany's rationing of food and the family's shortage of savings. Roentgen had contributed all of his personal fortune to good will.

To make matters worse, Bertha suffered a bronchitis attack that weakened her heart. She was unable to recover and died on October 31, 1919. Bertha's death after 47 loyal years of marriage was particularly difficult on her husband, who often carried on as if she were still alive. He would talk to her photographs and read her letters aloud. He even upheld a tradition of celebrating her birthday by eating the first asparagus of spring and picking violets for her.

As is typical in many close marriages, Roentgen did not live much longer after his beloved wife died. He retired from the university in 1920 at age 75, meanwhile continuing to use the university laboratory and to mountain climb. By the time he was 78, Roentgen was lonely and his body was tired. He suffered a short intestinal ailment and passed away several weeks later in Munich from carcinoma, or cancer, of the lower intestine. His death on February 10, 1923 caused the world to pause and recall the dedicated scientist who uncovered one of the greatest achievements of mankind.

Even after his death, Roentgen remained loyal to his principles. He requested the burning of all his scientific papers, personal writings and letters, perhaps due to his lifelong reluctance to record inaccurate information. He donated much of his remaining money to the city of Weilheim and a small amount to his vacation spot of Pontresina. He also left a fund to establish a Professor Doctor Roentgen Foundation to help educate poor students in his native city of Lennep. After all, Roentgen knew all too well the frustration of yearning for a seemingly out-of-reach education.

His will requested that his body be cremated, and his ashes buried in the same grave in Giessen with his wife and parents. The city still maintains the gravesite, keeping it covered with fresh flowers.

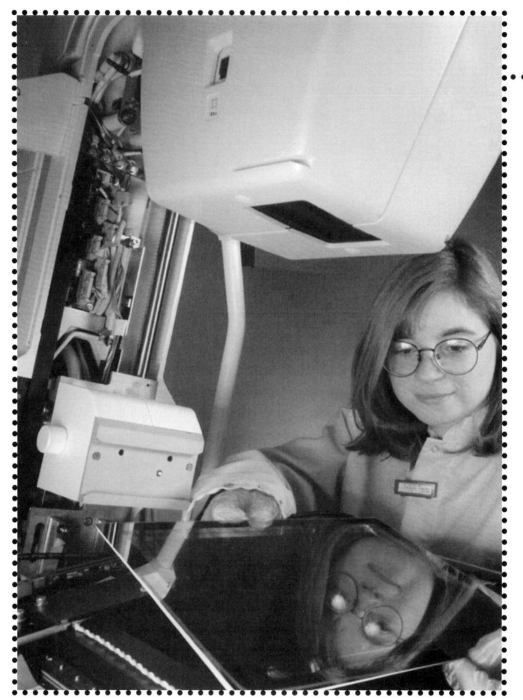

Modern day uses of x rays would have been well beyond Roentgen's imagination. In this photograph, GE Research and Development Center physicist Dr. Cynthia Landberg is testing a new digital x ray detector for GE Medical Systems. This is the first instrument to produce x ray images without film.

Chapter 6

Infinite Uses of X Rays

The use of x rays penetrates nearly every corner of modern life, in ways Roentgen never could have imagined. The discovery of x rays made way for advances in fields from medicine, science and industry to everyday areas, such as collecting valuables, mailing packages and protecting public safety. X rays have not just improved existing activities, but also led to the proliferation of new jobs and new machinery. Their potential has dazzled our imaginations, engaged us in challenging work, and left us forever appreciative of their infinite practical and life-saving uses.

Dr. H.S. Monell of New York reflected on his appreciation for x rays soon after their discovery by writing, "A new door has opened wide where none before was known to exist, and through it we may pass into a happier era, when uncertainty and empiricism shall give place to knowledge and definite therapeutics, and medicine shall take its rightful place among the sciences that are exact."

X rays are perhaps most miraculous in the area of medicine. Many doctors believe modern medicine would not be possible without x rays, which give them the ability to look inside the mysterious human body and to treat a variety of ailments. Their many medical uses include resetting bones, discovering the location of unwanted materials such as bullets or coins swallowed accidentally, studying the functioning of the body such as how the heart beats or digestion takes place, or locating tuberculosis, cancer and other deadly infections or growths.

In November of 1898, Dr. Leopold Freund was the first person to successfully use x rays to destroy an unwanted growth on the surface of a body. Freund used x rays to remove a disfiguring hairy mole on a little girl's neck and back. He gave the girl two hours of daily treatments for ten days. At that point, the hair fell out and was replaced by a small circular bald spot.

Friedrich Dessauer took the idea of using x rays to remove unwanted bodily growths a step further. He experimented with high voltages to determine how to remove growths deep in the body, such as cancer.

X rays had fascinated Dessauer since he first learned about them as a high school senior in Aschaffenburg, forty miles from Würzburg. He constantly experimented with machinery in his room, which he turned into a small physics lab and set to work on x rays shortly after learning about them. Dessauer eventually created a small portable x ray apparatus that helped diagnose his younger brother's lethal illness.

Years later, as a radiologist Dessauer visited Roentgen at his home during World War I to discuss his idea of using x rays to treat cancer. The two men had no way of knowing it then, but now the use of Dessauer's discovery can remove deep-seated carcinomas, such as the one in Roentgen's lower intestine that cost him his life.

Back then, the simplicity of x ray equipment limited medical applications of x rays. Early x ray machines were hot, noisy, slow, and dangerous. Some x rays took hours and their rays were more intense than necessary. Today, people use more precision regarding the intensity of x rays and protect themselves from the rays. Rooms lined with lead house x ray equipment, people wear leaded clothes to deflect the rays, and patients' actual exposure is measured in fractions of seconds rather than minutes.

Doctors also enjoy a wide variety of advanced x ray equipment, ranging from small portable machines to enormous ones that document parts of airplanes or spacecraft. X ray equipment today also is more versatile. Early machines took still two-dimensional pictures. X rays today include grid pictures of thick parts of the body such as hips or skulls, three-dimensional pictures that show organs inside a skeleton, or in-depth pictures that show how deep to make a surgical incision.

Contemporary x rays also record movement. Doctors can view moving x rays on videotapes, perhaps for consultation with colleagues, or on closed circuit television screens to monitor several patients at once.

In a closely related field, x rays have been equally helpful to dentists by enabling them to detect tooth decay early enough to prevent removing teeth. Before x rays, dentists could not detect decay until it was visible or the patient was in pain. At that point, removing the tooth was usually the only remedy. Today, dentists can see into a patient's teeth, jawbone and roots to find potential trouble spots long before the necessity of extractions.

Besides their uses in health-related fields, x rays have revolutionized industrial practices, particularly for manufacturers. X rays have improved product quality by helping manufacturers detect flaws. Roentgen himself was actually the first person to detect a flaw in a product by looking at an x ray. A picture of his shotgun revealed an air bubble in the metal of the barrel.

Manufacturers use a similar process today called non-destructive testing. Before x rays, manufacturers had to take a product apart to check for defects. Also, they were only able to inspect a few samples from a batch of products, so they had to assume that if the samples were useable, so was the whole batch. Manufacturers these days rely on automatic x ray systems that inspect products and reject substandard pieces without taking the product apart. The systems are able to inspect all products instead of just a few samples.

The military interests of the U.S. government went a long way toward advancing non-destructive testing. The U.S. government was first to institute systematic x ray testing in 1921 at the War Department Arsenal in Watertown, Massachusetts. The government installed a 200,000-volt Coolidge ray to inspect various war-related items. Previously, workers at the arsenal used a radiograph to inspect items. The U.S. government continued to expand its use of non-destructive testing during World War II to inspect everything from artillery shells to battleships.

Besides military uses, non-destructive testing has improved the quality of numerous everyday items. X rays can distinguish juicy oranges from dry ones. They can check the bonding of rubber to fabric in tires. They can find metal tacks inside boxed candy. They can detect fake collectibles, such as paintings, stamps, coins, even diamonds. Not to mention checking the quality of ship hulls, railroad tracks, automobiles, long-range missiles with 300,000 parts, wood, plastics and coal, even golf balls and porcelain eggs.

X rays have been particularly useful in improving the safety of aircraft so enormous that inspecting them any other way would be impractical. X rays enable mechanics to examine an airplane's wings, center section spars, skin and fittings, fuel lines and nozzles, and two to three layers of engine casings. They allow inspectors to look over thousands of parts inside the rockets and rocket motors that the U.S. used in moon explorations. X rays also assist in space navigation, laser science and astronomy. Rockets that take pictures in outer space have even revealed that some stars and the corona of the sun emit x rays.

The implications of x rays are staggering in many sciences. In palaeopathology, x rays have revealed information about ancient bone structure, injuries and diseases. In spectroscopy, x rays have provided valuable information about the composition of matter and chemicals, about catalysts for technical processes such as the cracking of crude oil, curing resins or hardening soft plastics, and about new elements that result from nuclear reactions. Even in Roentgen's former laboratory in Würzburg, scientists are hard at work measuring the polarization of x rays.

Today, Roentgen's name lives on among the almost infinite uses of x rays and a scattering of his namesakes around the world. His former laboratory is on a street renamed from Pleicher Ring to Roentgen Ring. The unit of the intensity of radiation is called one roentgen, or "R." Roentgenology refers to the field of medicine dealing with the diagnosis and treatment through x rays, and a roentgenologist is a doctor who works with x rays. Some German-speaking scientists even refer to x rays as "Roentgen rays."

These namesakes serve to remind us of a dedicated scientist who profoundly changed our world.

Chronology

- **1845**, born March 27 to Charlotte Constanze and Friedrich Conrad Roentgen in Lennep, Germany
- **1848**, moves with family to Apeldoorn, Holland
- **1864**, kicked out of the Technical School of Utrecht, losing his chance to gain a high school graduation certificate necessary to obtain a college degree in Holland.
- **1865**, enrolls at the University of Utrecht as a private student of philosophy to audit classes
- **1865**, becomes mechanical engineering student at the Federal Institute of Technology in Zurich, Switzerland
- **1866**, meets Bertha Ludwig in Zurich
- **1868**, graduates as mechanical engineer from Federal Institute of Technology
- **1869**, receives Ph.D. degree from the University of Zurich and becomes assistant there to Professor August Kundt
- **1872**, marries Bertha Ludwig in parents' Apeldoorn home
- **1872**, follows Kundt to University of Strasbourg to continue working as his assistant
- **1875**, becomes professor of physics and mathematics at the Agricultural Academy of Hohenheim
- **1876**, returns to University of Strasbourg as associate professor of theoretical physics
- **1879**, becomes professor of physics at University of Giessen
- **1887**, takes in six-year-old niece, Josephine Berta, and adopts her when she is 21
- **1888**, becomes professor of physics at University of Würzburg
- **1895**, discovers x rays
- **1896**, Vienna daily newspaper *Die Presse* breaks story of Roentgen's discovery
- **1900**, becomes professor of physics and director of physical science institute at the University of Munich
- **1901**, becomes first Nobel Prize winner for physics
- **1919**, wife dies in Munich
- **1920**, retires from the University of Munich
- **1923**, dies in Munich on Feb. 10

X Ray Timeline

- **1600**, Sir William Gilbert gives name of "electricity" to the same phenomenon found in lightning in his book *De Magnete*
- **1643**, Evangelista Torricelli discovers natural vacuum above a column of mercury in a glass tube that is induced by gravity
- **1672**, Otto von Guericke builds "electrical machine" to generate sparks
- early 1700s, Francis Haukesbee may have been first person to produce x rays when he observes a glow discharge during experiments with a vacuum tube
- **1700s**, Abbé Jean Nollet may have produced x rays while experimenting with an electrical egg
- **1794**, Alessandro Volta builds first electric battery
- **1838**, Michael Faraday notes that interior of a glass tube emptied of air glows when electricity is discharged between electrodes mounted at each end of the tube
- **1869**, Johann Wilhelm Hittorf discovers cathode rays
- **1875**, Sir William Crookes invents the Crookes Tube
- **1892**, Heinrich Hertz demonstrates that cathode rays can penetrate thin metallic foils made of gold, silver and aluminum
- **1894**, Philipp Lenard discovers that cathode rays can escape from a vacuum tube through a foil window; they disappear after traveling a few inches
- **1895**, German physicist Wilhelm Conrad Roentgen discovers x rays
- **1896**, French physicist Henri Becquerel's experiments with x rays lead him to discover radioactivity, a entirely new branch of physics
- **1897**, Sir Joseph John Thomson proves the existence of electrons
- **1900**, founding of American Roentgen Society, which quickly issues first warnings about dangers of excessive x ray exposure
- early 1900s, manufacturers began using non-destructive testing on products, which involves the use of x rays to check products for defects and to reject substandard pieces.
- **1916**, W.D. Coolidge patents Coolidge Tube, which has a truer vacuum than the Crookes Tube and is more stable and easier to control
- **1921**, War Department Arsenal in Watertown, Mass. implements first use of systematic x rays testing. The government installed a 200,000-volt Coolidge ray to inspect various war-related items
- **1936**, stone monument created at the Roentgen Institute in Hamburg, Germany to memorialize people who lost their lives to x rays exposure
- **1947**, ultrasound is used for medical purposes for the first time
- **1974**, Dr. Raymond Damadian receives patent for invention of the magnetic resonance imaging device (MRI)
- **1975**, Robert S. Ledley receives patent for diagnostic x ray systems, also known as CAT-Scans
- **1980**, first MRI imaging of human brain takes place
- **1997**, introduction of digital x rays

Further Reading

Esterer, Arnulf K. *Discoverer of X Rays: Wilhelm Conrad Röntgen.* New York: Julian Messner, 1968.

Gherman, Beverly. *The Mysterious Rays of Dr. Röntgen.* New York: Atheneum, 1994.

Glasser, Otto. *Wilhelm Conrad Roentgen and the Early History of the Roentgen Rays.* Novato, CA: Norman Publishing, 1993.

Grey, Vivian. *Roentgen's Revolution: The Discovery of the X Ray.* Boston/Toronto: Little, Brown and Company, 1973.

Kevles, Bettyann. *Naked to the Bone: Medical Imaging in the Twentieth Century.* Cambridge, MA: Perseus Press, April 1998.

McClafferty, Carla Killough. *The Head Bone's Connected to the Neck Bone: The Weird, Wacky, and Wonderful X Rays.* New York: Farrar Straus Giroux, 2001.

Mould, Richard F. *A Century of X Rays and Radioactivity in Medicine: With Emphasis on Photographic Records of the Early Years.* London, England: Institute of Physics Publications, 1993.

Murphy, Jack. *Nuclear Medicine (The Encyclopedia of Health).* New York: Chelsea House Publishing, 1993.

Nitske, W. Robert. *The Life of Wilhelm Conrad Röntgen.* Tucson, AZ: The University of Arizona Press, 1971.

Parker, Janice. Engines, *Elevators and X Rays* (Science at Work series). Austin, TX: Raintree-Steck Vaughn, 2000.

Skurzynski, Gloria. Waves: *The Electromagnetic Universe.* Washington, DC: National Geographic Society, 1996.

Winkler, Kathy. *Radiology* (Inventors and Inventions series). Tarrytown, NY: Benchmark Books, 1996.

Websites

American Roentgen Ray Society, www.arrs.org

Encarta Concise Encyclopedia, www.encarta.msn.com/index

High-Energy Astrophysics Learning Center, www.imagine.gsfc.nasa.gov/doc/people

Homeschool Fun!, www.homeschool!fun.com/sci.html

Internaut's Traveling Companion, www.shadow.net/~ebaumel/x_ray.html

National Atomic Museum, www.atomicmuseum.com/tour

NucNews, www.propl.org/nunews

Penn State University College of Medicine radiology department, www.xray.hmc.psu.edu/rci/ss4

Physics Calendar, www.northernsecondary.toronto.com

Radioactive Roulette, www.bergen.com/news/newatomic1999

ThinkQuest Library of Entries, www.libraryquest.org/13822

University of Illinois department of neurology, www.uic.edu/depts/mcne/founders

X Rays Century, www.emory.edu/X RAYS/century

Glossary

anode - positive terminal, or electrode, inside an electrolytic cell, vacuum tube or battery

carcinoma - malignant and invasive growth of tumor in the body, also known as cancer

caricature - a drawing of a person in which the facial features are distorted or exaggerated to produce a comical effect

cathode - negative terminal, or electrode, inside an electrolytic cell, vacuum tube or battery

cathode ray - a stream of charged particles traveling from the cathode to the anode

electricity - physical agency made up of tiny particles of electrons, protons and other charged particles.

electrode - conductor through which a current enters or leaves an electric or electronic device such as an electrolytic cell.

electrons - tiny particles that carry a negative charge and make up electricity

fluoroscope - tube or box fitted with a screen coated with fluorescent substance that uses x rays to view objects

Nobel Prize - one of the highest awards in the world, presented for extraordinary accomplishments in physics, chemistry, medicine, literature and contributions to world peace.

non-destructive testing - process of using x rays to detect imperfections in products in order to avoid taking them apart.

palaeopathology - study of disease of ancient times as inferred from fossil evidence

patent - government grant that gives an inventor the exclusive right to make, use and sell an invention for a specific period of time

polarization of x rays - the state in which x rays exhibit different properties in different directions

protons - tiny particles inside atoms that carry a positive charge and make up electricity

radiation - process in which energy is emitted by one body, transmitted through an intervening medium or space, then absorbed by another body

radioactivity - certain elements' spontaneous emission of radiation as a result in changes in the nuclei of that element's atom.

radiologist - person who studies x rays for medical uses

roentgenology - branch of medicine dealing with diagnosis and treatment of health problems through x rays

roentgenologist - doctor who uses x rays to diagnose and treat health problems

spectroscopy - study of the distribution of energy that a radiant source emits

tuberculosis - infectious disease that can affect any bodily tissue, particularly the lungs

vacuum tube - a sealed glass tube with two metal wires inside along which electrons travel

x rays - form of electromagnetic radiation similar to light but with shorter wavelengths and capable of penetrating solids and of ionizing gases

Index